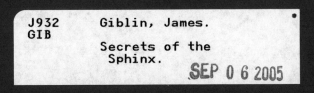

SECRETS OF THE SPHINX

BY

JAMES CROSS GIBLIN

ILLUSTRATED BY

BAGRAM IBATOULLINE

SCHOLASTIC PRESS   NEW YORK

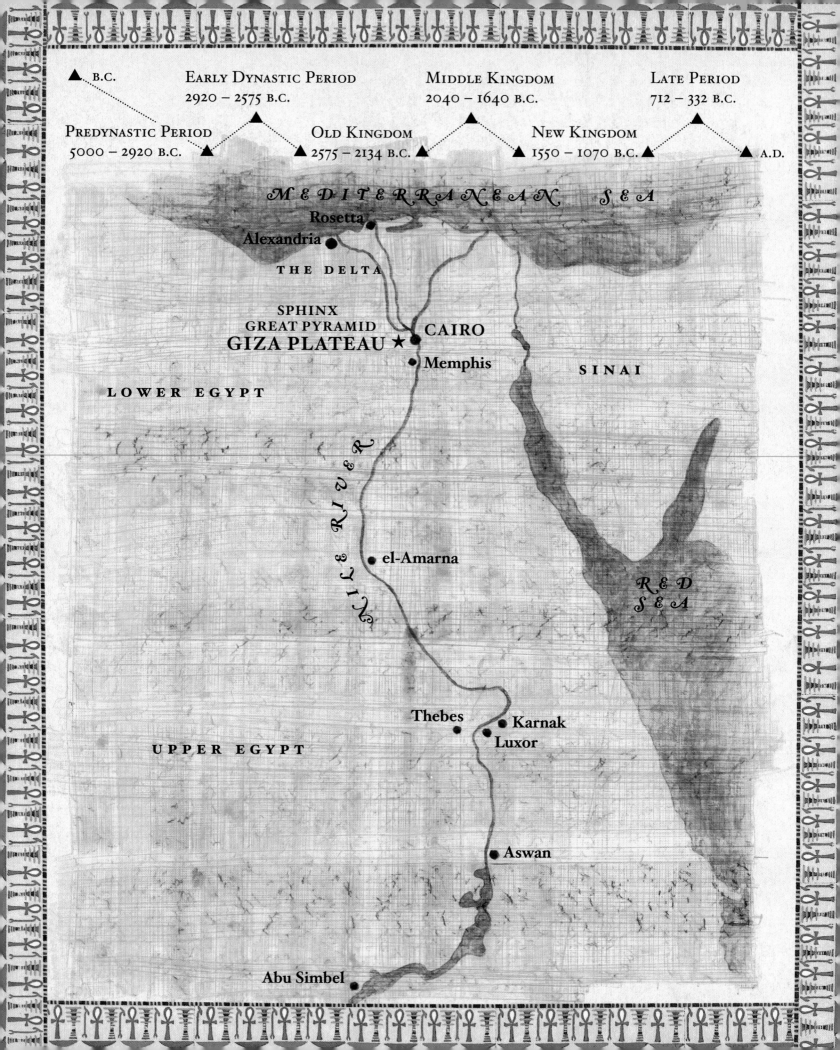

PREDYNASTIC PERIOD
5000 – 2920 B.C.

EARLY DYNASTIC PERIOD
2920 – 2575 B.C.

OLD KINGDOM
2575 – 2134 B.C.

MIDDLE KINGDOM
2040 – 1640 B.C.

NEW KINGDOM
1550 – 1070 B.C.

LATE PERIOD
712 – 332 B.C.

B.C.

A.D.

MEDITERRANEAN SEA

Rosetta

Alexandria

THE DELTA

SPHINX
GREAT PYRAMID
GIZA PLATEAU ★ CAIRO

Memphis

SINAI

LOWER EGYPT

NILE RIVER

el-Amarna

RED SEA

Thebes

Karnak
Luxor

UPPER EGYPT

Aswan

Abu Simbel

To the memory of Beatrice Creighton

— J. C. G.

To Dmitry Pogrebnov and Olga Evgrafieva

— B. I.

THE MYSTERIOUS CREATURE

Before dawn, the giant creature is almost invisible. It sits in shadow in its rocky, horseshoe-shaped hollow. Then, as the sun slowly rises in the east, the creature's body is gradually revealed.

First, the huge paws of a lion appear, followed by the animal's powerful haunches and shoulders. As the sun rises higher, the creature's face catches the light. But it is not the face of a lion. No, it is the face of a man. A man with broad lips, a broken nose, and eyes

headdress of an ancient Egyptian pharaoh.

This creature — part man, part beast — is the Great Sphinx. It was carved out of a natural rock formation, and is one of the largest sculptures in the world. From front to back, the Sphinx is the length of an average city block. It is as tall as a six-story building — sixty-six feet from its paws to the top of its head. Even its facial features are gigantic. What remains of the Sphinx's nose is more than 5 $\frac{1}{2}$

has a breadth of thirteen feet eight inches.

Behind the Sphinx, on the sandy Giza Plateau, stand three massive pyramids formed from blocks of limestone. The largest of the three, the Great Pyramid of Giza, covers an area large enough to accommodate ten football fields.

The three pyramids were built to house the mummies of pharaohs who ruled Egypt during the Fourth Dynasty, which lasted from 2575–2467 B.C. Scholars believe the Sphinx was carved at the time the second of the pyramids was erected. If they are

correct, the Great Sphinx has stood guard over this royal Egyptian cemetery for almost forty-five hundred years. That means it was already twenty-five hundred years old when Jesus was born.

Ever since the Sphinx was new, it has stared across the desert sands in the direction of the Nile River, a few miles to the east. Then, as now, the Nile was the vital backbone of Egyptian life, providing water for people, animals, and crops. But there was no city of Cairo on the banks of the Nile in 2500 B.C. This great city, the present-day capital of Egypt,

came into being much later.

Today, instead of open desert, the Sphinx looks out on souvenir stands and fast-food outlets. They stand less than two hundred yards away from the Sphinx's paws. These shops are part of the ever-expanding suburbs of Cairo, whose population has grown from two million to seventeen million in just forty years. With this growth have come cars, sewage, and air pollution, all of which have created problems for the Sphinx and the pyramids.

Other problems are brought on by the hordes of tourists from all over the world who visit the Giza Plateau each day. The money the tourists spend is essential to the health of the Egyptian economy, but their tramping feet and sweaty hands can cause

damage to the ancient monuments.

Still, the tourists come, as they have since the days of the ancient Greeks and Romans. They gaze in awe at the Great Sphinx and the pyramids, and ask their guides the same questions visitors to Egypt have always asked: Who built these structures, and why? What do they mean? And how did their builders, using primitive tools, ever manage to shape and carve such towering monuments?

The answers to those questions aren't simple, and many of them have yet to be found. For to understand the pyramids and the Sphinx, one must first travel back to a time long before they were built — a mysterious time before there were any written records — a time before history.

THE BEGINNINGS OF EGYPT

No one knows exactly who the ancient Egyptians were. Nor is it known how they arrived at the long, narrow strip of fertile land along the Nile River that became their home. But by about 5000 B.C., Egypt had developed a flourishing Stone Age culture. These people chipped flints for knives and ax blades; made clay pots; grew crops of wheat and millet; and kept cows, goats, and donkeys.

The descendants of these people built on the accomplishments of their forebears. They discovered metals and made weapons and tools out of copper. They learned how to weave cloth, how to

paint and sculpt, and how to add and subtract. At life's end, they buried their dead in rectangular graves lined with mud brick. No buildings from this period survive because they, too, were built of mud brick that crumbled long ago. But stone statues of lions, their mouths open in snarls, have been found in excavations of some ancient Egyptian ruins. The statues may have stood guard outside temples and inspired the sphinxes of later times.

Two important events occurred in the next phase of Egypt's development, starting about 3100 B.C. A pharaoh, whom some scholars call Narmer and others call Menes, united northern and southern Egypt into one nation and established his capital at Memphis.

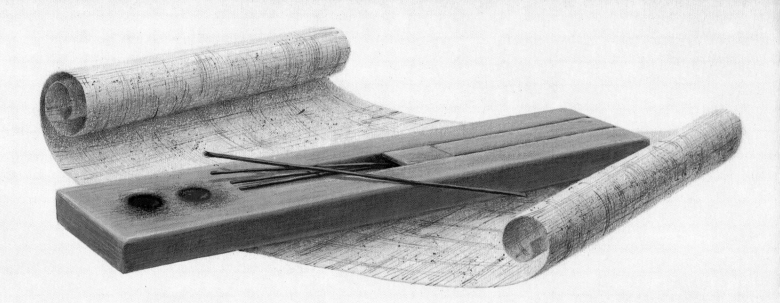

The city rose along the banks of the Nile, a few miles south of present-day Cairo. The other event was of equal, if not greater, importance: The Egyptians learned to write. When that happened, they left the shadowy world of prehistory and entered the world of history.

For a long time, scholars thought that the Sumerians, who lived in what is now Iraq, invented writing. The Sumerians made wedge-shaped marks in wet clay tablets that were then baked. This type of writing is called *cuneiform*, which means "wedge-shaped."

The ancient Egyptians traded with the Sumerians, and may have exchanged ideas about writing with them. But the Egyptians did not use wedge-shaped marks in their writing. Instead, they created a set of symbols called *hieroglyphs*. Scholars now believe that the earliest examples of hieroglyphic writing, dating to about 3500 B.C., are older than the earliest examples of cuneiform writing.

Egyptian hieroglyphs were difficult to under-stand and to copy, so only a small number of people learned how to write. They were called *scribes*, and occupied a position of honor in ancient Egyptian society. The scribes carved the hieroglyphs on stone monuments or wrote them on sheets of papyrus, a paperlike material made from a tall plant which still grows in abundance along the Nile. Sheets of papyrus were glued together in rolls from which a scribe would cut off as much as was needed for a letter or document. Scribes wrote on the papyrus with a reed pen, using an ink made of water, gum, and soot.

Almost none of the earliest papyrus texts survive, and only a few of the oldest stone inscriptions remain. For information about the earliest periods in Egyptian history, scholars must rely on the accounts of later writers and the discoveries made by archaeologists. From these sources, the scholars have been able to piece together a list of the pharaohs who governed Egypt during the first dynasties. (A dynasty is a succession of rulers who are members of the same family).

LIFE AFTER DEATH

Religion was central to Egyptian life from the beginning, and the pharaoh played a key role in its rituals. In life, the ruler was thought to be the son of Ra, the all-powerful sun god. In death, he rejoined his father in the west, the place where the sun set. There, in the Egyptian afterworld, he would enjoy eternal life, but only if his earthly body was still intact.

This led to the ancient Egyptian practice of mummification, the attempt to preserve the body after death by embalming it with resin, sodium carbonate, and other chemicals, and wrapping it in fine linen gauze. Originally, only the pharaoh, his queen, and other members of the royal family were mummified. Later, the practice spread to include high government officials and other people of means. Later still, the Egyptians embalmed cats, dogs, horses, cows, hawks, and other animals that were sacred to them.

Monumental tombs were built to house the royal mummies and everything they would need for life in the hereafter — clothes, jewelry, chairs, beds, dishes, even food. The first tombs, called *mastabas*, were flat-roofed structures with sloping sides of mud brick. By the Third Dynasty, the royal architects had begun to erect more permanent structures made of stone. The most noteworthy of these was the first Egyptian tomb that resembled a pyramid — the so-called step pyramid of the pharaoh Zoser, which rises in six ever-smaller terraces to a height of one hundred ninety feet.

The next dynasty, the Fourth, witnessed an incredible flowering of Egypt's civilization. There were fresh advances in the fields of mathematics, medicine,

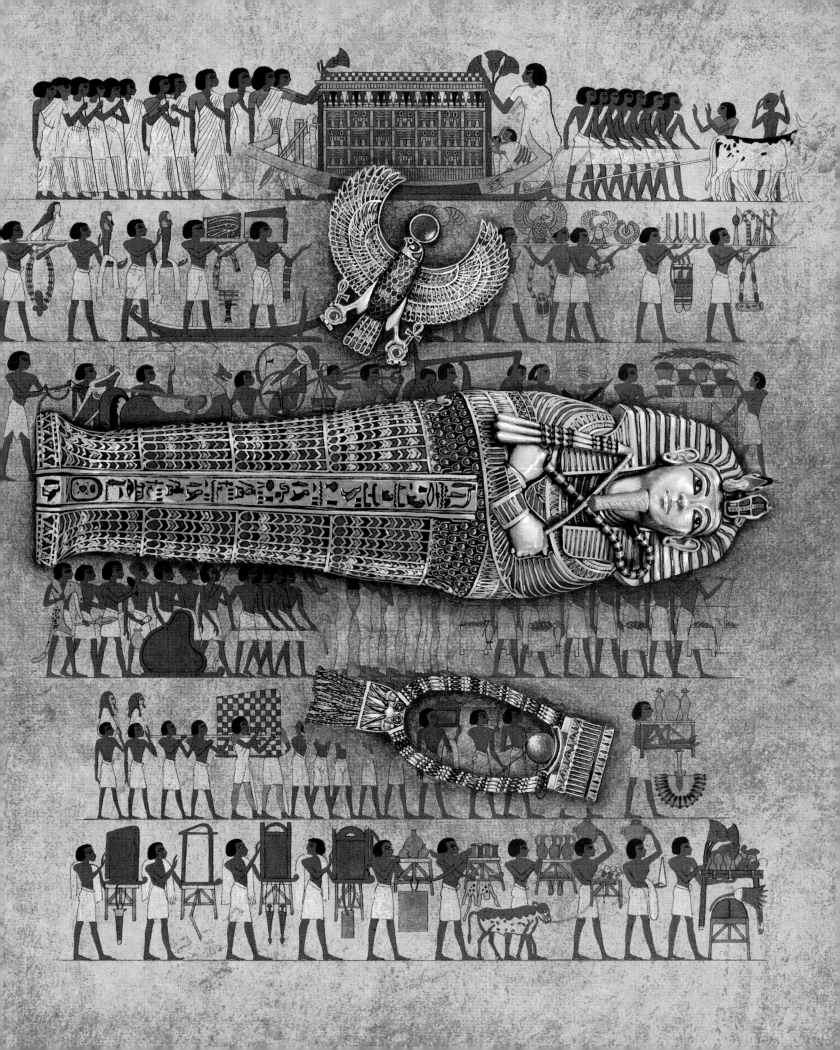

literature, and astronomy. Most spectacular of all were the strides made in architecture. These included the structures that rose on the Giza Plateau: the three huge pyramids and the Great Sphinx. More than one hundred other pyramids would be built in Egypt during later dynasties, but none of them would be as massive as the Giza tombs. Nor would any of the later sphinxes be as impressive as the Great Sphinx. It proved to be one of a kind.

The development of the pyramid can clearly be traced from the one-story mastabas of the First Dynasty to the towering structures at Giza. The path that led to the Great Sphinx is much less obvious. Other than a small sphinx with a woman's face that may have been carved during the reign of the previous pharaoh, no earlier examples have been found.

The lion had long been a symbol of strength and power in ancient art, but the sculptors of the Great Sphinx were the first, as far as we know, to combine the animal's body with the head of a man.

This was not just any man. Many scholars are convinced that the face on the Sphinx is actually a portrait of the Egyptian ruler Khafre, for its features closely resemble statues of him. Moreover, Khafre was one of the pharaohs who ruled Egypt during the Fourth Dynasty, and the pyramid immediately behind the Sphinx contained his remains.

Almost nothing is known of Pharaoh Khafre, who was called Chephren in Greek. But if he was even partly responsible for the creation of the Great Sphinx and the other achievements of the Fourth Dynasty, he deserves to be immortalized on the sculpture's face.

Perhaps the discovery of other sphinxes from earlier dynasties, or of written texts describing them, will reveal more of the Great Sphinx's secrets. In the meantime, archaeologists digging in the earth near the Sphinx and the pyramids have uncovered some startling new facts about how the monuments were built and the lives of the ancient Egyptians who labored on them.

CREATORS OF THE SPHINX

Until recently, scholars thought the builders of the pyramids and the Sphinx must have been little more than slaves. They believed the unfortunate workers were forced to labor on the monuments under threat of torture — or worse. Lately, however, a very different picture has emerged as a result of excavations on the Giza Plateau.

The foundations of row upon row of mud-brick houses have been unearthed at one of the sites. Scholars think that some of them were the homes of the overseers who supervised the building crews. Others were probably the residences of the skilled craftsmen who sculpted the face of the Sphinx and decorated the royal chambers in the pyramids.

It is estimated that five hundred to one thousand craftsmen lived with their families in the workers' settlement. These specialists devoted most, if not all, of their working lives to the design and construction of the Sphinx, the pyramids, and the temples and smaller tombs that surrounded them. From the available evidence, the craftsmen were respected for their abilities and lived well by ancient Egyptian standards.

Near the mud-brick houses, archaeologists have discovered the remains of a number of barracks-like buildings. Scholars believe these were the dwellings of the unskilled laborers who helped to build the pyramids and the Sphinx. The laborers were probably young farmers who were drafted to work on the monuments during the months when they were not needed to plant or harvest the crops. At any given time, it is thought there were five to seven thousand such laborers living in the military-style barracks at Giza.

As work on the pyramids and the Sphinx continued, the settlement grew to be the size of a city. Besides dwelling places, it had production and storage facilities for food, fuel, and metal tools. There was a building where fish caught in the Nile were dried and salted for future use. And there were bakeries in which bread — the staple of the workers' diet — was made from emmer, a form of wheat. It tasted like sourdough bread.

There was also a cemetery where those who died during the construction of the pyramids were buried. Domes built of limestone blocks marked the graves of the overseers and skilled craftsmen in the upper part of the cemetery. The common laborers were buried in the lower part of the cemetery under smaller domes made of mud brick.

None of the workers were mummified, but when scientists unearthed their graves they found many skeletal remains. These added to the scientists' knowledge of the conditions under which the pyramid builders labored, and the medical treatment they received.

Somewhat surprisingly, males and females were represented almost equally in the graves. This suggests that women played a bigger role in the construction of the pyramids and the carving of the Sphinx than anyone had previously imagined.

Life expectancy was much shorter in the ancient world than it is in most places today. The skeletons of the male workers indicate that many of them died between the ages of thirty and thirty-five. More females than males died before the age of thirty, which probably reflects

the hazards of childbirth in ancient times.

The remains of both the men and women show signs of hard labor. Severe arthritis of the back and the knees was found in many skeletons, probably the result of constant heavy lifting. Other skeletons bore evidence of fractures in arms and legs. However, most of the fractures had healed completely, with full realignment of the broken bones. This indicates that the workers were given good medical care, and that the fractures were set with splints. It also reinforces the notion that the men and women who labored on the Giza Plateau were treated humanely.

Still, their work was extremely hard. Equipped only with hammers, chisels, and axes, they cut huge blocks of granite and limestone from quarries far and near. Then they transported the blocks to the building site by boat and sledge, and raised them into place as the pyramids gradually took shape. The Great Pyramid alone is composed of two million, three hundred thousand individual blocks of limestone, each of which weighs about two and one-half tons. The entire structure weighs approximately six and one-quarter million tons!

A RED FACE, A BLUE BEARD

Carving the Great Sphinx presented a different set of problems and took months, if not years, to complete. It was shaped out of a rock formation in the middle of a quarry from which the limestone blocks for Khafre's pyramid had been cut. First, someone with the eye of an artist must have noted a resemblance between the formation and the body of a lion. Then that artist — or more likely, a team of artists — had to make a plan for sculpting the Sphinx from the rock.

The men and women responsible for shaping the head and face must have worked on shaky platforms rising fifty or sixty feet above the ground. No doubt some of them suffered falls resulting in broken bones like those found in the skeletons in the Giza cemetery. Once their fractures had healed, most of them probably took up their hammers and chisels once more. Their skills would have been needed as work continued on the giant sculpture.

There are three distinct layers of limestone in the Sphinx. The bottom layer, from which the front paws and hind legs were carved, is firm and hard. But the layer above it, which forms most of the lion's body, is much softer. Fortunately, the third layer, from the neck up through the head, is hard again. This explains why the Sphinx's facial features have survived so well for thousands of years even though its body has been severely damaged by weathering.

When the Sphinx was carved, it had a braided beard, only traces of which remain. From the center of its headdress reared the figure of a cobra or asp. These snakes were sacred in ancient Egypt and symbolized the pharaoh's great power. The Sphinx today is mainly varying shades of beige, the color of the original limestone from which it was made. But traces of red can be seen here and there, indicating that it was once painted. Scholars believe that when the creature was new, its face and body were red. Its beard, eyebrows, and the stripes in its headdress were probably blue, while the rest of the headdress was bright yellow.

All the structures on the Giza Plateau looked very different in ancient times. Long stone

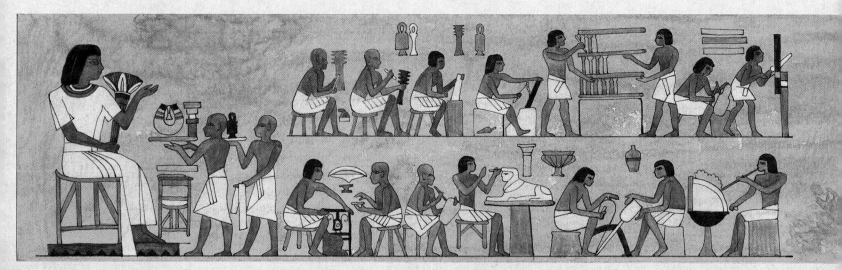

causeways lined with statues led from the banks of the Nile up to the three pyramids. There was a pillared temple at the beginning of each causeway, and another temple at the foot of each pyramid. The pyramids themselves were covered with slabs of polished white limestone that gleamed in the sunlight in honor of the sun god, Ra. Smaller pyramids for queens and tombs for high officials surrounded the Great Pyramid on three sides. And guarding them all was the brightly colored Sphinx, stretched out in its stone hollow.

Shortly after the Giza complex was completed, the building of pyramids suddenly became less important in Egypt. No one knows exactly why. Perhaps the kingdom's human and material resources had become exhausted. The Great Pyramid alone had taken twenty-three years to erect and had required the services of at least one hundred thousand people. Whatever the reason, Giza marked the high point of Egyptian pyramid construction. The pharaohs who came later would build magnificent tombs for themselves, but none of these would equal the colossal structures on the Giza Plateau.

Many sphinxes would also be carved in the future. Some of them were set like guards on either side of the entranceway to a temple or palace. Others were placed in rows bordering the main avenues that led to these buildings. Most of these sphinxes had human heads like the Great Sphinx, with faces that bore the features of whoever was pharaoh at the time. But some were carved with a ram's head or the head of a hawk. Human- or animal-headed, these sphinxes all symbolized the power of the Egyptian gods and the pharaoh. But none of them was as large or as imposing as the Great Sphinx.

Around 2000 B.C., the capital of Egypt moved south from Memphis, which was near Giza, to Thebes. The monuments on the Giza Plateau were neglected. Thieves broke into the pyramids in search of treasure and looted the nearby temples. Winds swept in from the desert, gradually covering the Great Sphinx with sand.

Hundreds of years passed while the Sphinx lay half-buried. Then, one day in 1400 B.C. or thereabouts, a young prince named Thutmose happened upon the creature. And like an ancient Sleeping Beauty, the Great Sphinx awoke to a bright new life.

THE SPHINX IS REDISCOVERED

The story of Prince Thutmose and his encounter with the Sphinx soon became a legend in Egypt. Audiences young and old delighted in hearing storytellers recount it, and scribes wrote it down for later generations to read and enjoy. Here is how the tale went:

The young prince was hot and tired. He had been hunting lions and gazelles in the desert near the Giza Plateau since early morning. Now it was nearly noon, and he still had not brought down any animals with his javelin.

In the distance, the prince saw a stone head rising up out of the sand. He knew it was the Sphinx, carved more than one thousand years before at the command of one of his ancestors. Beyond the head, a welcome patch of shade stretched across the sand. The prince swung his horse-drawn chariot around and headed toward it. Shade was a rare and precious thing in the treeless desert.

The prince lay down to rest in the Sphinx's shadow and almost immediately fell asleep. And in his sleep he heard a voice — the voice of the Sphinx itself. It spoke to him like a father to his son, and this is what it said: "Oh my son Thutmose, I am your father, the god of the sun. I shall give to you my kingdom, and you shall wear its crown. To you shall belong the earth in its entire length and breadth, and to you shall be apportioned the great products of every foreign country."

While the prince listened in awe, the voice of the Sphinx went on. "But behold, I am ailing in all my limbs and my entire body is in pain. For the sand of the desert presses in upon me from every side. I am waiting for you to do what must be done, for I know that you are my son and my champion. Approach; I am with you; I shall be your guide. . . ."

At that point, according to the legend, the prince awoke. But he was still conscious of the Sphinx's words and determined to do something about the statue's plight.

We will probably never know how much of this legend is true. But it *is* true that as soon as Thutmose became pharaoh in 1401 B.C., he ordered that the sand surrounding the Sphinx be cleared away completely. Now the giant creature was revealed once more in all its strength and majesty.

Thutmose did not stop there. He directed his royal craftsmen to patch with mortar and stone the places where wind-driven sand and erosion had worn away the Sphinx's body. And he had the story of how the Sphinx had spoken to him carved on a large stone slab. The slab was set in place between the Sphinx's paws where everyone who approached the creature could see and read it.

As one century followed another, thousands of Egyptians and people from other countries came to visit the Sphinx. Some of them admired the creature, like the Roman author Pliny, who wrote in the first century A.D., "In front of the pyramids is an even more wonderful work. It is regarded as a divinity by the local people. They maintain that it was brought there from a distance, but the truth is that it was carved from natural rock. For religious reasons, the face is painted red."

Others menaced it, like the Arabs from the Near East who conquered Egypt in the seventh century A.D. The Arabs, who were Muslim, tried to get the Egyptians to embrace the Muslim faith. They removed the white facing stones on the pyramids and used them in constructing the bridges, towers, and mosques of their new capital city, Cairo.

The Sphinx was too big to dismantle. But when the Arabs realized that some Egyptians still worshipped it, they decided to do something to weaken the statue's influence. First, the Arabs launched a campaign of words against the Sphinx, calling it the "Father of Terrors." Then some Arab fanatics got busy with their hammers and chisels and knocked off the Sphinx's nose and part of its upper lip.

The fanatics thought the damage would make the Sphinx unrecognizable, but many Egyptians still came to bow in prayer before it. After the Arabs disfigured the statue, sand blew onto the fields near Giza, causing the crops to fail. The Egyptians hoped their prayers to the Sphinx would lift this curse from the land.

Eventually, the farmers cleared their fields of sand, but the Sphinx itself was gradually buried once more. Travelers from Europe saw only its battered head, and legends sprang up about the mysterious creature. One legend spread by a sixteenth-century German visitor, Johannes Helferich, may have been inspired by the story of Thutmose's dream. "Under the ground, through a narrow hidden passage beneath the Sphinx, one can pass unseen," Helferich wrote. "By this passage the heathen (Egyptian) priests get inside the head and speak to the people out of it as if the statue itself had spoken."

Visitors like Helferich had little solid information about the Sphinx because no one could read the hieroglyphic writing of the ancient Egyptians. The meaning of the hieroglyphs had been almost completely lost over the centuries. But a way to decipher the hieroglyphs was about to be found. With it, scholars would be able to go beyond legends and guesswork and get a grip on the actual history of Egypt — including the history of the Sphinx.

THE ROSETTA STONE

In 1798, the French general Napoleon Bonaparte invaded Egypt with an army of thirty-eight thousand soldiers, and set out to gain control of that country for France. Along with his army, Napoleon brought more than 150 French scholars, artists, and scientists to Egypt.

The scholars studied the hieroglyphic writings they found everywhere, but made little headway in deciphering them. Meanwhile, a group of French soldiers stationed near the town of Rosetta had unearthed a stone slab with writing on it in three different languages. When the scholars saw the slab, they realized this could be the clue they'd been searching for.

The writing was a royal decree. It had been etched onto the slab in the mysterious hieroglyphs, in another kind of Egyptian writing called *demotic*, and in Greek. The scholars made copies of the writing on the slab by covering it with printers' ink, laying sheets of paper on it, and pressing down on the sheets with rollers to obtain good, clear impressions. Some of the copies went to France, others to England. Experts in both countries compared the Greek and hieroglyphic versions of the decree, word by word and symbol by symbol.

Several of the experts came close to deciphering the hieroglyphs, but failed in the end. Then a brilliant young French linguist, Jean-François Champollion, tried his hand at the task. Comparing the hieroglyphs on the Rosetta Stone with those of another Egyptian inscription, he managed to

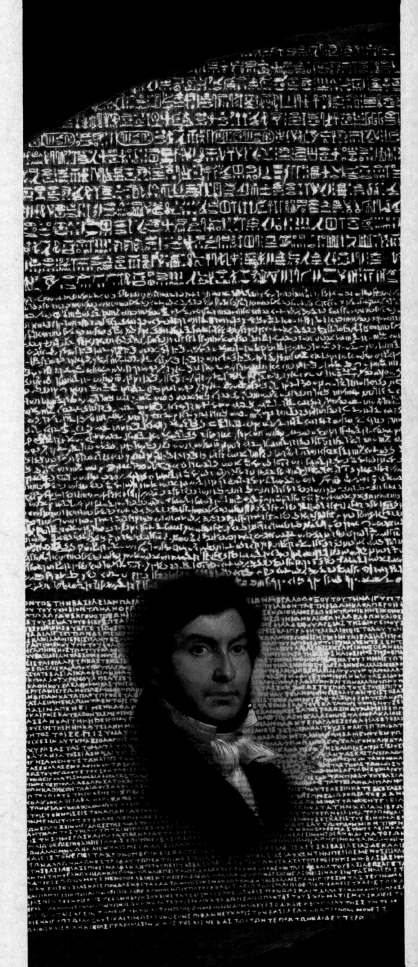

decipher the names of two rulers, Ptolemy and Cleopatra. Now he knew the meaning of a dozen different hieroglyphic symbols. Building on that base, he went on to decipher many other Egyptian names and words.

Other scholars made use of Champollion's discoveries and translated one piece of Egyptian writing after another. Among them was the writing on the slab that Thutmose had placed in front of the Sphinx. Unfortunately, some of the text had worn off over the years. But the section that was left stated that the Sphinx had been carved during the reign of a much earlier pharaoh. The first part of his name followed: Khaf. The rest of the name was missing.

In the meantime, scholars had found other texts that listed the early pharaohs in sequence. From them, the scholars discovered that a pharaoh named Khafre was one of those who had ruled Egypt in

the Fourth Dynasty. Further evidence indicated that the second pyramid on the Giza Plateau — the one directly behind the Sphinx — had been built for Khafre. Putting these discoveries together, the scholars decided that the Sphinx, too, had been constructed during Khafre's reign. They announced that it had probably been carved about 2500 B.C.

Most experts on ancient Egypt accepted this dating for the Sphinx. And later archaeological discoveries seemed to support it. For example, when the quarry in which the Sphinx sits was cleaned thoroughly in the late 1970s, scientists found fragments of Fourth Dynasty tools and pottery in a crack in the floor. They also excavated hammer stones made of diorite that were used during the Fourth Dynasty to smooth the limestone. "All this stuff was obviously left by the people who built the Sphinx," one of the scientists said.

But some geologists rejected this evidence. They challenged the date of 2500 B.C. for the Sphinx, and claimed that it had been carved much, much earlier — sometime before 5000 B.C., in fact. As proof of their theory, the geologists cited the way the body of the Sphinx had eroded over the centuries.

The accepted view was that wind-driven sand from the Sahara Desert had brought about the rippled pattern on the Sphinx's midsection. The geologists were not convinced. They believed that only heavy rainfall could have caused the severe erosion of the Sphinx. Yet all the available evidence indicated that the Sahara, which once was covered with lush grasslands, had dried up sometime between 6000 and 5000 B.C. After that time, there were few heavy rains in Egypt. Thus, according to geologists, the erosion of the Sphinx's body must have occurred well before 5000 B.C., and the statue must have been carved even earlier than that.

The geologists' theory raised a number of new questions about the Sphinx. It also won the support of those who believed the history of ancient Egypt had followed a very different course from the one outlined by scholars. These people accepted the geologists' earlier date for the Sphinx, and went on to speculate that it may not have been carved by the ancient Egyptians at all!

According to their interpretation of Egyptian history, the Sphinx and the pyramids behind it were the work of priests and scholars from an even older and more advanced civilization located on the lost continent of Atlantis. When disaster struck the continent, many of its highly educated inhabitants managed to escape. They found their way to Egypt about 10,500 B.C. and began to create what we think of as the wonders of Egyptian civilization — including the Great Sphinx.

THE LEGEND OF ATLANTIS

The notion that Atlantis had a strong connection to ancient Egypt was not new. It originated in the mind of Edgar Cayce, an eccentric American who lived from 1877 to 1945. Cayce's disciples have kept his ideas alive, and have founded the Edgar Cayce Foundation to promote them.

As a young man, Cayce suffered from an impediment that made speech almost impossible. He sought help from one doctor after another, but none of their treatments worked. Then one day Cayce discovered that he could put himself into a deep trance. During the trance, he somehow managed not only to diagnose his ailment, but also to prescribe a remedy for it.

Word of Cayce's cure spread, and he found himself in great demand as a faith healer. He toured the United States, performing thousands of what he called "life readings." After meeting a patient, Cayce would go into one of his trances and then begin to speak. An assistant took down everything he said about the patient's physical condition and future prospects. When Cayce woke up, he had no

recollection of what had happened during the trance . . . or so he claimed.

Cayce was a firm believer in reincarnation, and his "life readings" often focused on his patients' former selves. Many of them, Cayce said, had once lived on the fabled continent of Atlantis. And so had he. Cayce claimed to be the reincarnation of the high priest of Atlantis, Ra-Ta. Along with hundreds of his fellow Atlanteans, Ra-Ta had managed to escape the destruction of his homeland, and had found his way to Egypt's Nile Valley in the eleventh millennium B.C.

Edgar Cayce did not invent the idea of the lost continent called Atlantis. Its story was told for the first time by the Greek philosopher Plato in his *Dialogues,* written in 345 B.C. According to Plato, the continent was situated in the Atlantic Ocean beyond the "Pillars of Hercules" (the Straits of Gibraltar). Atlantis was a large island, bigger than North Africa and the Middle East combined. Its rulers had built their land into a rich and powerful empire, and had erected a magnificent capital city

along the coast. At its center, decorated with silver and gold, stood a temple to Poseidon, god of the sea.

The people of Atlantis were well-educated but warlike, Plato said. They had already conquered part of North Africa and Europe and were planning an attack on Greece when disaster struck suddenly. In about 10,000 B.C., according to Plato, the huge island was hit first by a tremendous volcanic eruption and then by a tidal wave and flood. Hundreds of thousands of its inhabitants were killed, and the entire continent sank beneath the sea.

The destruction of Atlantis makes a dramatic story, but there's no evidence that it ever occurred. Nor is there any evidence that Atlantis itself was a real place. Many scientific investigations have been conducted on the Atlantic Ocean seafloor. These indicate that there never was a large island-continent out in the Atlantic beyond the Straits of Gibraltar. In addition, no advanced civilization like that described by Plato is known to have existed anywhere in the world as far back as 10,000 B.C.

The sad story of Atlantis may have been inspired by what happened to the Mediterranean island of Crete. The highly developed civilization on Crete collapsed suddenly and without explanation around 1500 B.C. At about the same time, the volcanic island of Thera, sixty-five miles north of Crete, erupted violently. The eruption caused tremendous devastation throughout the region. In its wake, a giant wave battered Crete, destroying all of the island's harbors and every town and palace along its shores.

Refugees from Crete spread tales of the island's destruction in Egypt and elsewhere. Along the way, the tales probably became more and more fanciful. By the time Plato heard them, it's likely they no longer concerned events that had happened on Crete. Instead, the tales had probably been transformed into accounts of the destruction of another island — the long-lost continent of Atlantis.

Many people in Plato's time accepted his version of the story, though. So do a considerable number of people today, despite all evidence to the contrary. Mythical creatures like the unicorn and the abominable snowman, and mythical places like Atlantis, have always had a broad appeal.

BENEATH THE SPHINX'S PAWS

One of the staunchest believers in Atlantis was Edgar Cayce. Not only did Cayce think he was the reincarnation of its high priest, Ra-Ta, but he also believed that he was one of the refugees from Atlantis who had helped to build the pyramids and the Sphinx. Moreover, Cayce said during several of his trances that the Sphinx was far more than just a statue. He claimed that Ra-Ta and his fellow priests had chosen it as the hiding place for the priceless documents they had brought with them from the lost continent. These books and papers recounted the history of Atlantis, its religious beliefs, and the secrets of its advanced civilization. They were buried, Cayce said, in an underground chamber between the Sphinx's paws.

Cayce gave specific directions on how to reach the chamber, which he called the Hall of Records. Speaking in the voice of Ra-Ta, he said, "There is a passage from the right forepaw of the Sphinx that descends to the entrance of the record chamber." He went on to predict that the Hall of Records would be discovered and entered at or just before the end of the twentieth century.

Edgar Cayce died more than fifty years ago, but his followers remain faithful to his beliefs. Starting in the late 1970s, the Edgar Cayce Foundation funded several scientific investigations in Egypt. The goal of these investigations was to prove that Cayce's visions were accurate. Researchers placed electrodes in the ground around the Sphinx to detect any empty spaces in the rock below. When they discovered signs

of several such spaces, they drilled down into the rock. But they found nothing except natural irregularities. One of the researchers described them as "cavities that looked like the holes in Swiss cheese."

The followers of Cayce did not let this failure stop them. Instead, they joined forces with the geologists who were attempting to prove that the Sphinx had been eroded in the distant past by heavy rains. In 1993, they helped to sponsor a television special, watched by more than thirty-three million Americans, that advanced the geologists' erosion theory and the Sphinx's supposed link with Atlantis. They also backed the explorations of a scientist who claimed to have found indications of a large rectangular chamber in the bedrock between the paws of the Sphinx.

At this point, representatives from the Egyptian Antiquities Organization stepped in. First, they put a stop to all probes and drilling in the area around the Sphinx, fearing it might undermine the statue. They went on to denounce the activities of the Cayce Foundation and its supporters as frivolous and unscientific.

Cayce's followers protested the ban on further probes. But Dr. Zahi Hawass, director of the Giza Pyramids Authority, defended the action. He cited all the evidence showing that no continent like Atlantis had ever existed. As for the theory that only heavy rains could have eroded the Sphinx, Dr. Hawass noted that many other processes of erosion might account for the weathering patterns on the statue. For example, sand wetted by occasional rains or river floodwater could have eaten into the softer limestone of the Sphinx's body.

Above all, Dr. Hawass and other Egyptian experts pointed out that there was absolutely no archaeological evidence to support the notion that the pyramids and the Sphinx were constructed as far back as 10,500 B.C. At that period in human history, people in Egypt and elsewhere were still using simple flint tools and roving the earth in small groups. For food, they fished, hunted wild animals, and gathered nuts, fruits, and edible roots. Farming was not practiced in Egypt until 5000 B.C. at the earliest.

The early Egyptians lived in caves or temporary shelters made of branches and animal skins. They did not begin to build mud-brick dwellings until much later. In fact, no permanent settlements or towns are known to have existed in Egypt before about 3500 B.C. So how could people living in the area in 10,500 B.C. have constructed the pyramids from huge blocks of

stone? Or carved the massive face of the Sphinx?

These arguments seemed logical to most people, but the followers of Edgar Cayce refused to be swayed by them. Going on the attack, they flooded Egyptian government offices with new requests to drill around and underneath the Sphinx in search of Cayce's Hall of Records. His followers were convinced a message of tremendous impotance would be found there — perhaps the key to the deepest secrets of the universe.

While Cayce's followers continued to press their case, Dr. Hawass and his colleagues were trying to deal with a far more urgent matter. The modern world, with all its problems, was getting closer and closer to the monuments on the Giza Plateau. If ways weren't found to protect the pyramids and the Sphinx, they might suffer irreparable damage.

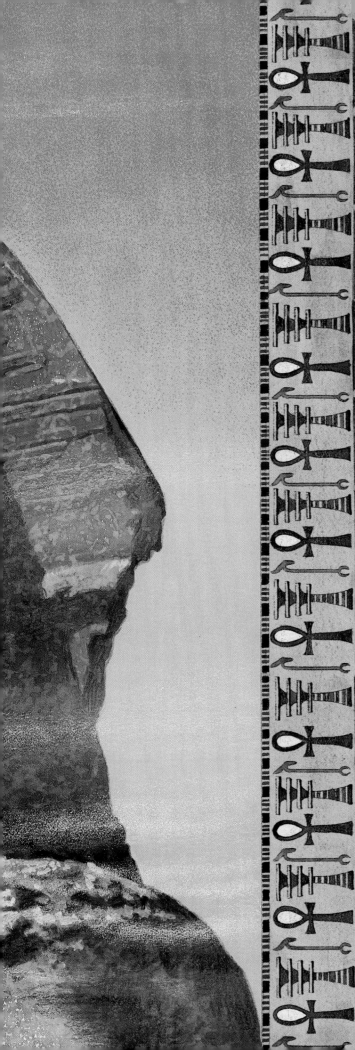

PROTECTING THE SPHINX

Almost every day, slices of limestone the size of potato chips flake off from the body of the Sphinx. If there's a breeze, they float away on it. Otherwise, they drop to the ground.

Scientists aren't sure what can be done to prevent the flaking. It's caused by salt deposits within the limestone. Moisture condenses on the Sphinx during the cool of the night and the early morning hours. This dampness draws the salt to the surface, where it dissolves. But the salt crystallizes again when the dew burns off in the heat of the day. Then the salt crystals expand and push at the statue's surface, causing the top layer of stone to flake off.

This continuous deterioration is most noticeable in the soft limestone of the Sphinx's chest. Some scientists have suggested that the chest be injected with chemicals to strengthen and stabilize the stone. Others would like to encase the chest in limestone panels. But no one knows what negative side effects chemicals might have on the stone. Nor does anyone know how the new panels would affect the original stonework underneath. Not to mention the fact that additional panels would drastically change the appearance of the Sphinx.

There is more agreement on how to deal with the chunks of rock breaking off the Sphinx. Ever since the time of Thutmose IV, decayed or fallen sections of the statue have been replaced with fresh slabs of limestone. But some of these repairs have been more effective than others. And a few of them —

including some recent alterations — have ended up doing more harm than good.

After a large piece of rock fell from the Sphinx's left hind paw in 1981, a major restoration effort was begun on the lower part of the statue. Workers from the Egyptian Antiquities Organization removed the eroded slabs from earlier repairs and replaced them with new, larger stones. The replacements halted further accidents for a time. But by 1987, the new slabs had begun to slip and buckle outward, perhaps because of moisture coming from the core stones beneath. Then, in 1988, a sizable chunk of replacement stone fell from the Sphinx's right shoulder.

All further work on the repairs was stopped while the authorities evaluated the situation. Eventually, they decided the only thing to do was to strip away all the repairs made since 1981 and start over. This time, smaller slabs would be used in order to achieve a tighter fit. They would also be easier to replace if any of the slabs began to deteriorate.

Until recently, scientists could only guess at the effect the environment was having on the Sphinx. Then, in 1990, the Getty Conservation Institute in California designed a solar-powered monitoring station that was put in place behind the statue. It measures the direction and speed of the wind on the Giza Plateau, as well as the relative humidity and the degree of air pollution. The people involved in restoring the Sphinx made good use of this information as they proceeded with their repairs.

Scaffolding went up around the giant statue in 1990. Workers stood on it to remove the eroded stones from earlier restorations and replace them with brand-new slabs. More than one hundred thousand new slabs were used in the operation, which took seven years to complete. The workers did not touch the damaged face of the Sphinx, however. Like earlier restorers, they decided it would be too risky to tamper with its familiar expression.

At last, the job was finished in December of 1997. The scaffolding came down, and a festival was held in the spring of 1998 to celebrate the restoration of the Sphinx's lower body. Families from Cairo and tourists from all over the world gathered at the base of the statue. While balloons floated overhead, the visitors gazed in awe and delight at the ancient monument, its fresh, new stonework gleaming in the sun.

THE FUTURE OF THE GREAT SPHINX

Unfortunately, the restoration doesn't mean that the threats to the Sphinx are over. Cairo's expanding suburbs keep getting closer to the Sphinx and the pyramids. Air pollution levels remain high, and Cairo's smog now ranks among the worst in the world. Plans to build a ring highway around the Giza Plateau have been canceled for the moment because of protests, but they may be revived. If the highway is built, the view of the open desert beyond the Sphinx will be lost for good.

Some experts believe that only extreme measures can safeguard the Sphinx from the environmental dangers that menace it. One proposal would seal the statue off from the world by covering it with a glass pyramid. Another would protect it with a flexible shelter on rails that could be rolled into place when needed, and rolled back when the danger receded. The most drastic suggestion is to rebury the Sphinx in sand!

It's doubtful that any of these far-out solutions will be adopted. What's more likely to save the Sphinx is the same thing that has preserved other historic sites, from the towering rocks at Stonehenge, England, to the Statue of Liberty in New York City, to the oldest houses in many small American towns. That's the steady, patient, unceasing concern of everyone who cherishes such treasures.

Meanwhile, the search for answers to the mysteries of the Sphinx goes on. How and when was its midsection eroded? What ceremonial role did the statue play in the religious rituals of the ancient Egyptians? Most intriguing, why was it the only giant Sphinx with a human face that the ancient Egyptians ever carved?

Answers to these and other such questions probably won't come from ongoing attempts by the followers of Edgar Cayce to locate a Hall of Records beneath the Sphinx's paws. Chances are the answers will emerge instead as a result of some future archaeological excavation. Perhaps those digging down into the remains of a royal tomb will happen upon a papyrus scroll or a stone slab that contains hitherto unknown information about the Sphinx and its secrets.

Until that day arrives, however, scholars and other interested parties will have to content themselves with the simple fact that the gigantic statue is still standing guard on the Giza Plateau. It has already endured for more than forty-five hundred years. With a little luck, and the continuing support of those who value it, the Great Sphinx should be able to gaze at the dawn for at least a thousand more.

A Different Kind of Sphinx

The idea of the sphinx spread from Egypt to other parts of the ancient world. Wherever it traveled, the sphinx remained a symbol of strength and power. Its appearance underwent many changes, however. In Mesopotamia, its lion's body acquired the wings of an eagle. And in Greece, where it was first portrayed in art about 1500 B.C., the sphinx's human features were those of a woman.

The Greek sphinxes' heads were covered with long, elaborate wigs, and wings swept back from their shoulders in graceful curves. A smile often graced a Greek sphinx's lips, but that didn't mean that she was a kindly creature. Quite the contrary, in fact. Most Greek stories about sphinxes depicted them as having a cruel nature. This was certainly true of the most famous sphinx in Greek literature — the one who appears in the classic drama, Oedipus, the King.

The Sphinx in Oedipus had a beautiful face but the heart of a monster. She perched all day on a tall rock, looking down on a road that led to the royal city of Thebes. Whenever a traveler passed by, the Sphinx asked the person the following riddle: "What walks on four legs in the morning, on two legs at noon, and on three legs in the evening?"

If the traveler couldn't answer the riddle, the Sphinx swooped down from her perch, grabbed the person by the neck, and strangled the unfortunate man or woman to death.

This went on for years, until the area on both sides of the road became littered with human skeletons. Then, one day, Oedipus came striding along the road. The Sphinx gave him her treacherous smile and asked in a sweet voice, "Tell me, young man — what walks on four legs in the morning, on two legs at noon, and on three legs in the evening?"

Without hesitating, Oedipus answered, "A man. He crawls on his hands and feet when he's a baby; he walks on two good legs in the prime of his life; and he has to use a cane when he's old."

The Sphinx's face crumpled in disbelief and anger. Oedipus had done what no one else had been able to do. He had succeeded in answering the riddle! The Sphinx hurled herself into the air, then plummeted onto the jagged rocks below. When Oedipus clambered over the rocks to examine her, the monstrous creature was dead.

Thus ended the legend of the best-known Greek sphinx. It bore almost no resemblance to the sphinx that inspired it — the giant statue that still sits on Egypt's Giza Plateau.

Source Notes and Bibliography

THE FOLLOWING BOOKS AND ARTICLES WERE ESPECIALLY HELPFUL IN MY RESEARCH. THEY ARE LISTED HERE IN ORDER OF IMPORTANCE.

RIDDLES OF THE SPHINX by Paul Jordan (New York: New York University Press, 1998). Provides thorough coverage of when and how the Sphinx was built, the purposes it may have served, and the forces that have buffeted it over the centuries.

THE MESSAGE OF THE SPHINX by Graham Hancock and Robert Bauval (New York: Crown Publishers, Inc., 1996). Echoing the theories of Edgar Cayce, the authors propose an earlier construction date for the Giza pyramids and the Sphinx, and speculate on the message that may lie buried beneath the statue.

"THE SPHINX: WHO BUILT IT, AND WHY?" by Zawi Hawass and Mark Lehner (article in *Archaeology* magazine, SEPTEMBER/OCTOBER, 1994). The Egyptian scientist in charge of the restoration of the Sphinx and an American professor of Egyptology recount the history of the Sphinx and current efforts to preserve it.

"BUILDERS OF THE PYRAMIDS" by Zawi Hawass and Mark Lehner (article in *Archaeology* magazine, JANUARY/FEBRUARY, 1997). Drawing on information gained from recent excavations, Hawass and Lehner develop a picture of the men and women who constructed the Giza pyramids and the Sphinx, and the conditions under which they lived and worked.

OTHER BOOKS AND ARTICLES THAT PROVIDED USEFUL INFORMATION INCLUDE:

LIFE IN ANCIENT EGYPT by Adolf Erman, translated by H.M. Tirard (New York: Dover Publications, Inc., 1971).

THE WHITE GODDESS by Robert Graves (New York: Farrar, Straus & Giroux, 1966, 1976). Compares Egypt's Great Sphinx with the sphinxes of other cultures.

A DICTIONARY OF EGYPTIAN GODS AND GODDESSES by George Hart (London and New York: Routledge & Kegan Paul, Inc., 1986).

THE WORLD OF THE PHARAOHS by Christine Hobson (New York: Thames and Hudson, 1987).

EGYPTIAN MYTHOLOGY by Veronica Ions (New York: Peter Bedrick Books, 1990). Includes an account of the mythological significance of the Sphinx.

"SPHINX IS POKER-FACED, BUT IS IT SITTING ON A SECRET?" by Douglas Jehl (article in *The New York Times,* MAY 24, 1997). Discusses the pros and cons of drilling to find out if there is a message from the ancients buried under the Sphinx's paws.

THE PHARAOHS OF ANCIENT EGYPT by Elizabeth Payne (New York: Random House, 1964). An informative introduction for ages eight to twelve.

ANCIENT EGYPTIAN MYTHS AND LEGENDS by Lewis Spence (New York: Dover Publications, Inc., 1990). Offers information about the symbolic meaning of the lion in ancient Egyptian art and literature.

WHEN EGYPT RULED THE EAST by George Steindorff and Keith C. Seele (Chicago and New York: The University of Chicago Press, 1942, 1957). Contains an account of the gradual burial of the Sphinx and its unearthing by Pharaoh Thutmose. Included is a description of the dream the young pharaoh had when he fell asleep at the foot of the Sphinx.

"PERILS OF THE SPHINX" by Alexander Stille (article in *The New Yorker,* FEBRUARY 10, 1997). Summarizes contemporary threats to the Sphinx from the environment and a steady flow of human visitors.

THE TRAVELER'S KEY TO ANCIENT EGYPT by John Anthony West (Wheaton, Illinois, and Madras, India: Quest Books, 1995). Describes the position of the Sphinx and pyramids today, surrounded by the fast-growing suburbs of Cairo.

Index

BOLDFACE PAGE NUMBERS REFER TO PICTURES.

LIBRARY OF CONGRESS CATALOGING-IN-PUBLICATION DATA

Giblin, James Cross.

Secrets of the Sphinx / by James Cross Giblin; illustrated by Bagram Ibatoulline.— 1st ed.   p.   cm.

Summary: Discusses some of Egypt's most famous artifacts and monuments, including the pyramids, the Rosetta Stone, and, especially, the Great Sphinx, presenting research and speculation about their origins and their future.

ISBN 0-590-09847-0 (alk. paper)

1. Great Sphinx (Egypt)—Juvenile literature. [1. Great Sphinx (Egypt) 2. Sphinxes (Mythology) 3. Egypt—Antiquities.

4. Egypt—History.] I. Ibatoulline, Bagram, ill. II. Title. DT62.S7 G53 2004   932—DC22   2003019666

10 9 8 7 6 5 4 3 2 1   05 06 07 08

Printed in Mexico 49   First edition, October 2004

The illustrations were done in gouache and water color.

The text was set in Hoefler Text Roman. ▲ The display type was set in Hf LaVardera Book.

Book design by Marijka Kostiw

Special thanks to Edward Bleiberg, Ph.D., Associate Curator, Egyptian, Classical, and Ancient Middle Eastern Art, Brooklyn Museum of Art, for his meticulous fact checking of text and art.